A PICTORIAL HISTORY OF THE F-117 NIGHTHAWK

Published by

Lloyd Leslie

The F-117 Nighthawk was developed by Lockheeds secret SKUNK WORKS division in response for the need for a jet fighter that could operate completely undetected by the enemy. The Nighthawk was the first to be built around stealth technology and was based on the Have Blue stealth demonstrater.It was developed rapidly and in complete secrecy.

The F-117'S first flight took place in 1981 but was kept secret from the public until 1988

64 F-117s built, with 5 of those being prototypes and 59 were production versions

known as the "Stealth Fighter" it played an active role in 1990-1991 Gulf war.The only Nighthawk to be lost in combat was shot down by a SAM Missile in Yugoslavia in March 1999.

Its pilot, Lt. Col. Dale Zelko was rescued by the Air Force combat search and rescue team.

Lockheed F-117A Nighthawk - 81-10798 flying over the Sierra Mountains

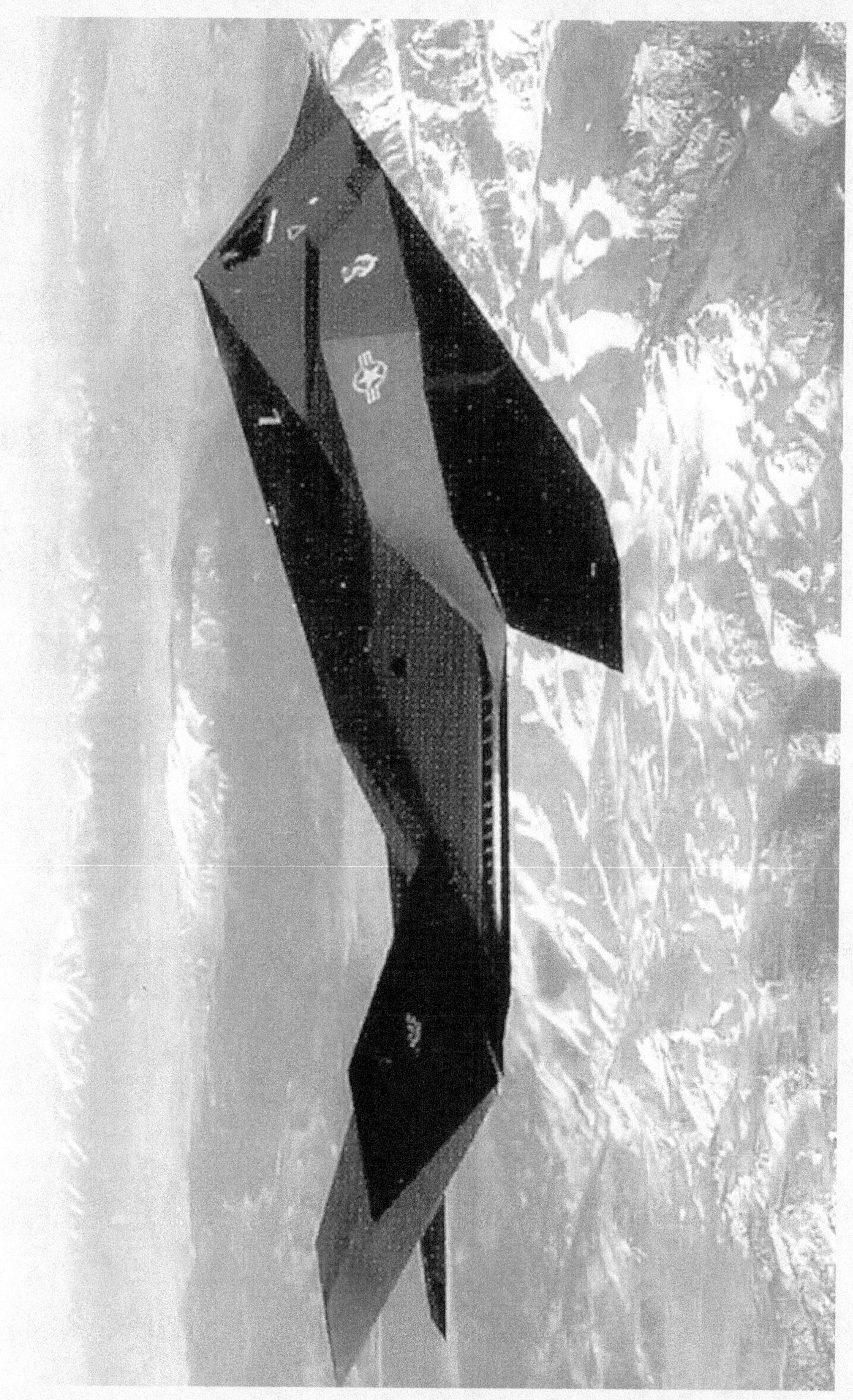

F-117A Nighthawks of the 49th Operations Group at Holloman AFB, after the re-designation of the 37th Fighter Wing

F-117 NUMBERS
Crew:1

F prefix denotes Fighter

B is for Bomber

A is for Attack aircraft

Length: 65 ft 11 in (20.09 m)

With room for just two bombs, the F-117's "F" prefix was a misnomer. Technically speaking, it should have been the B-117 (bomber) or A-117 (for attack aircraft).

Wingspan: 43 ft 4 in (13.21 m)

A pair of specially painted F-117 Nighthawks fly off from their last refueling by the Ohio National Guard's 121st Air Refueling Wing.

Height: 12 ft 5 in (3.78 m)

F-117A making a flyover of Holloman AFB, New Mexico

Wing area: 780 sq ft (72 m2)

An F-117 Nighthawk engages its target and drops a GBU-27 guided bomb unit during the 'live-fire' weapons testing mission

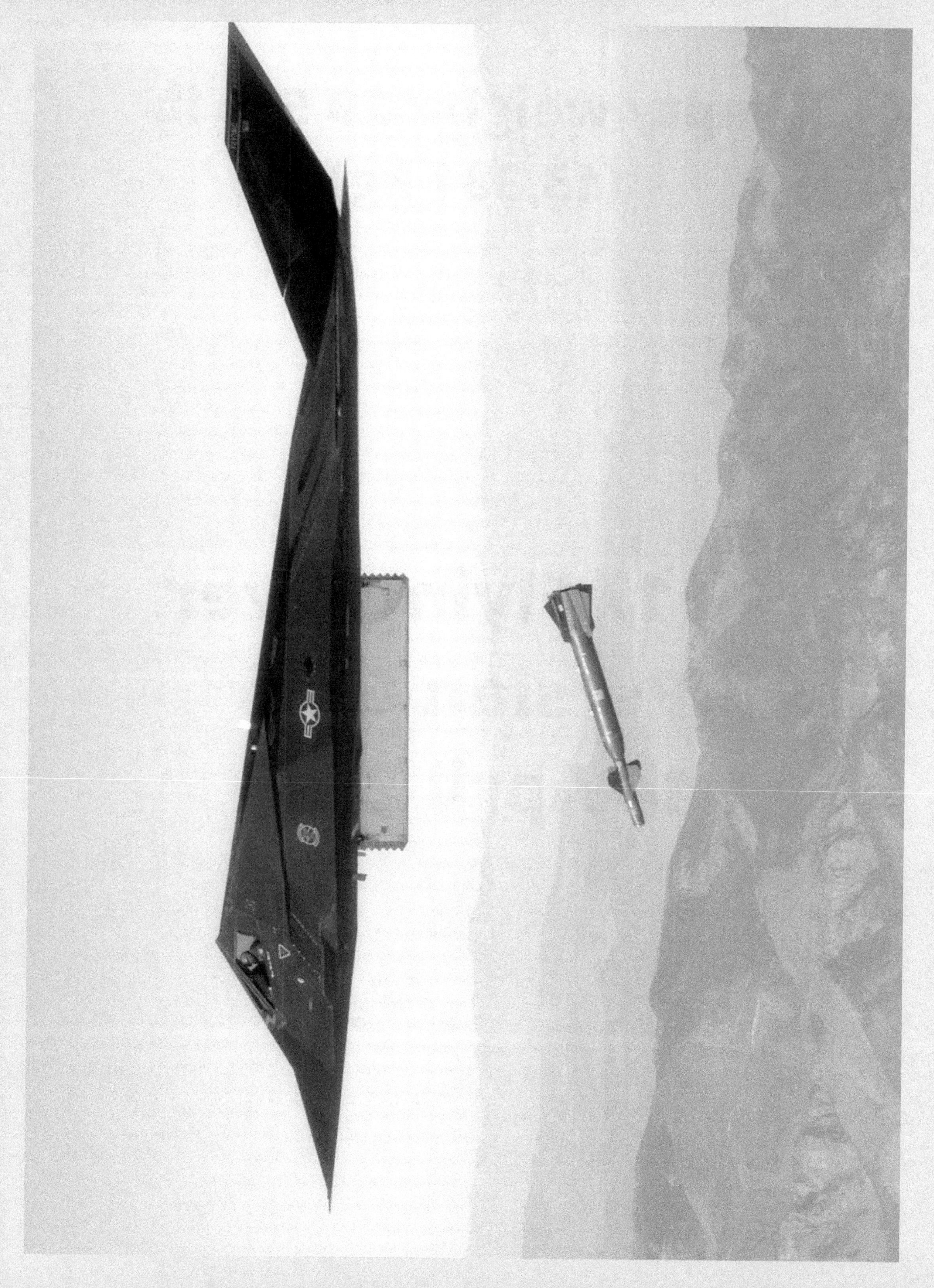

Empty weight: 29,500 lb (13,381 kg)

F-117 Flying Over Persian Gulf 14 April 2003

Max takeoff weight: 52,500 lb (23,814 kg)

F-117A Nighthawk Stealth Fighter aircraft flies over Nellis Air Force Base

Powerplant: 2 × General Electric F404-F1D2 turbofan engines, 10,600 lbf (47 kN) thrust each

2 × internal weapons bays equipped to carry bombs

8th Fighter Squadron F-117A 86-0838 taxing by a Wright "B" Flyer during the US Air and Trade Show at Dayton International Airport, 17 July 2003

Maximum speed: 594 kn (684 mph, 1,100 km/h) Mach 0.92

An F-117 Nighthawk with a T-38 Talon chase plane flying over Tonopah

Range: 930 nmi (1,070 mi, 1,720 km) unlimited with aerial refuelling

Lockheed F-117A Nighthawk Persian Gulf 1996

Price per aircraft:US$42.6 million (flyaway cost) US$111.2 million (average cost)

25 stealth fly over the Tularosa Basin as part of the Silver Stealth celebration Oct. 27, 2006, at Holloman.

Service ceiling: 45000 ft (14,000 m)

F-117A Nighthawk leading a formation of Royal Saudi Air Force aircraft over the desert

F-117 Nighthawks fly on one of their last missions

B-2 Spirit Bomber and F-117 Nighthawk in Formation

An F-22 Raptor, an F-117 Nighthawk, an F-4 Phantom and an F-15 Eagle fly over Holloman Air Force Base, N.M., Oct. 27, 2007

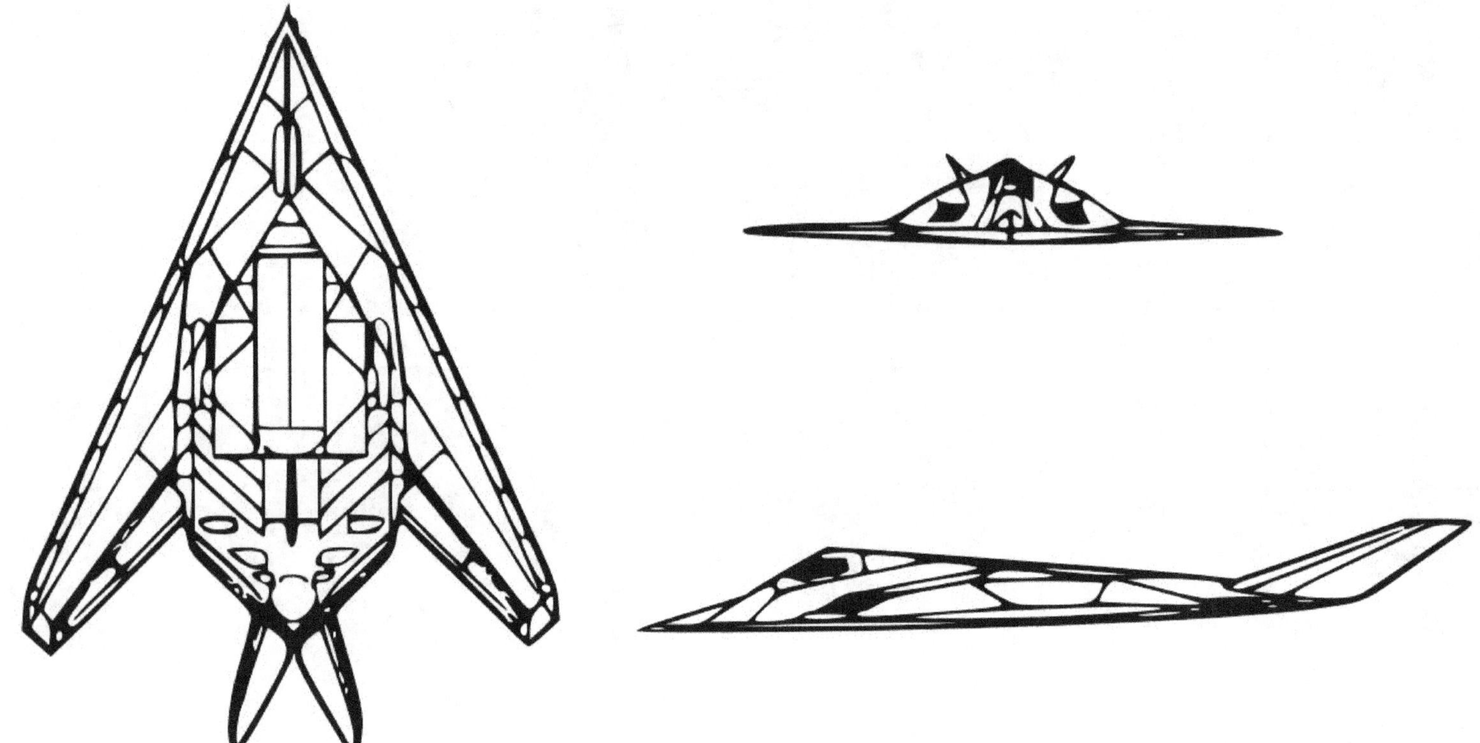

F-117 cockpit

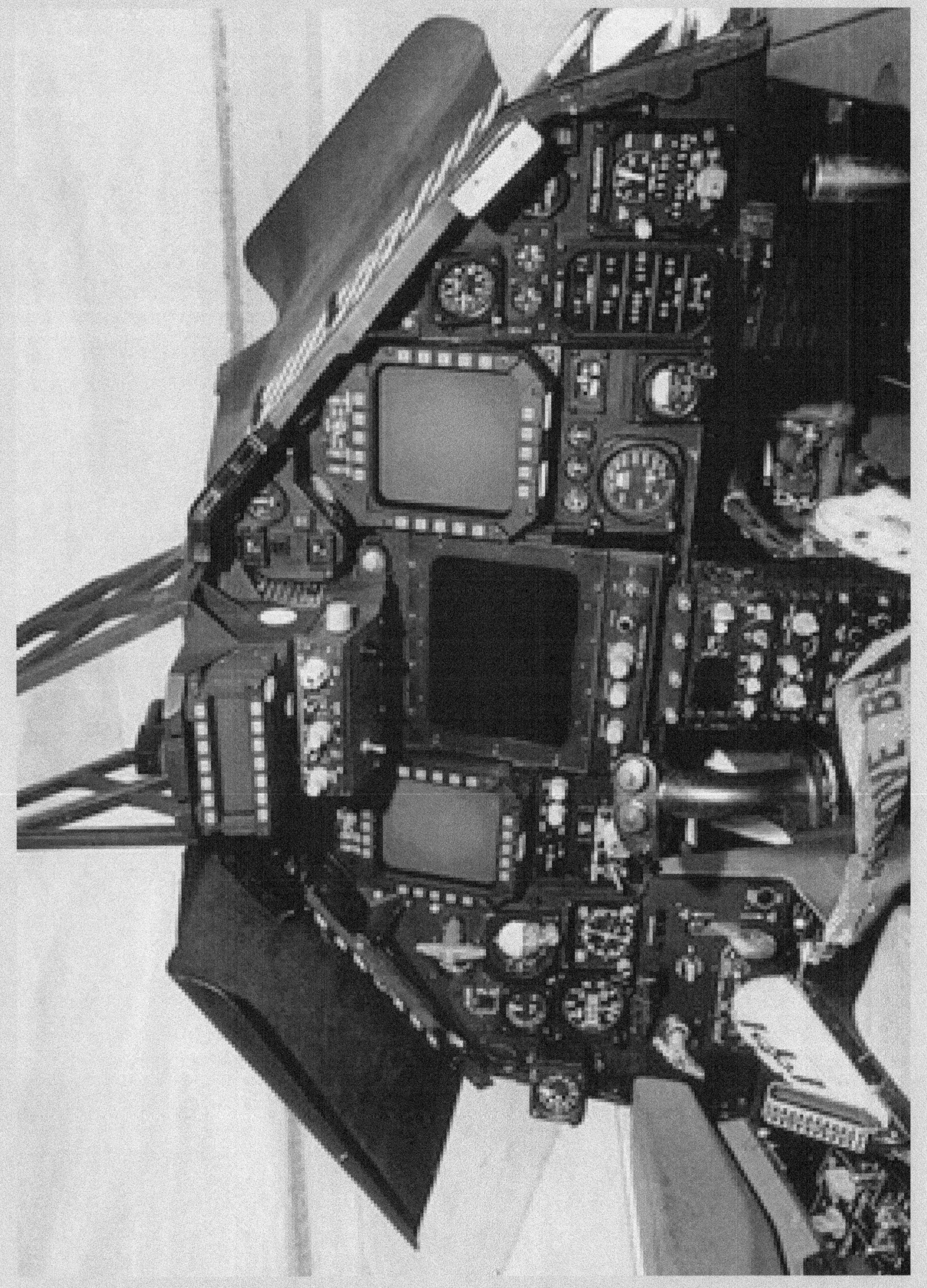

410th Flight Test Squadron - F-117 Formation

Lockheed F-117A Nighthawk 79-7082 in experimental grey motif. Later, this motif was used by the Air Force on the F-22 Raptor

The Air Force retired the F-117 on 22 April 2008, primarily due to the acquisition and eventual deployment of the more effective F-22 Raptor .

The F-22 programme was cancelled in 2009 and replaced with the cheaper and more versatile F-35 Joint Strike Fighter.

But even in retirement it wasn't the end for the world's first stealth combat aircraft. All 52 F-117s were retired into a form of storage where they were kept in near-airworthy condition just in case a conflict broke out and America once again needed to call on the F-117

THE END